It All Belongs

The Law of Attraction and Nature of the Universe

Also by Teresa Griffith

Love Your Skeletons
York Boat Captain—18 Life-Changing Days on the Peace River
Forging Sisterhood in the Frozen North

In the **Tiny Books on Big Ideas** series:
Intelligence is Everywhere — Looking at Animals, Vegetables, and Minerals
Two Trees — Attitudes that Lead to Wellness
Togetherness — Healthy Friendships, Relationships, and Communities
Tiny Books on Big Ideas, Volume 1

It All Belongs

The Law of Attraction and Nature of the Universe

Teresa Griffith

Tiny Books on Big Ideas - Book 1

Cover design and typography by Teresa Griffith
Available for print-on-demand at Lulu.com

teresagriffith.ca

ISBN 978-0-9921204-1-2

In gratitude and appreciation

for the giants

whose shoulders I stand upon.

Contents

Acknowledgements

You may have heard that writing a book is a labour of love. While it may be labour for some, for me, it is play. I am happiest when I am indulging in one of my creative outlets and I love to write, so the greater hardship would be keeping all these ideas in. It does take time, however, and many tasks such as yard work, weeding the garden and doing the dishes did suffer while I focused on finishing these tiny books. For his patience, literary suggestions, editing skill and most of all, his unbelievable love, I must thank my husband, Darren Griffith. He is so dear to me, and I know that this series would not have been as easy without his help, nor would the quality of the finished product be as high.

I must extend special thanks to all my lovely friends in Edmonton and sprinkled around Alberta. Thank you so much for all your encouragement, smiles, hugs and acceptance. I love you all!

Two friends I met when I lived up north have been invaluable in giving feedback and suggestions to the final draft. Michelle Clarke, thank you for everything. There is no doubt in my mind that these tiny books are better thanks to you. I would love to thank Tim Brown for all the deep conversations. To all my many other northern friends, I appreciate and love you more than you know!

Lastly, I must acknowledge my phenomenal family. I am who I am in large part because of the foundation you gave me. You continue to shower me with love and acceptance, along with practical help and good advice. My dad, Rudy Kneller, my mom, Donna Kneller and my sisters, Patricia and Gina, I love you and appreciate you so much.

If we could change ourselves, the tendencies in the world would also change. As a man changes his own nature, so does the attitude of the world change towards him. ... We need not wait to see what others do.

- Gandhi

Introduction

I went for a walk one winter day in the bush on our land. It was crisp and cool out, and I made my way between the trees, through snow a little deeper than my ankles. I meandered along, gradually making my way to an area I call Rose Hill, where wild roses abound in summer. The snow had a crust here, so I walked on top of the snow drifts for a while. On my way back to the house, I went past our second dugout. It's like a small pond between the hay field and the bush.

The dugout was frozen over of course, and as I looked back, I noticed something peculiar. I thought I saw a flower pattern in the ice, like that of a hibiscus flower. I looked again and saw hibiscus flower patterns all over the ice. How could this be? Why would frost form in the shape of flowers? My brain struggled with the reality of what I was seeing. It was amazing and impossible at the same time. I had been thinking about my hibiscus tree earlier that day. And now, there were blossom patterns on the ice.

This is just one of many events in my life that leads me to say *there is so much more going on than we realize.* We humans can be so obtuse, thoroughly unobservant, and wrapped up in ourselves. We often take metaphors and myths literally. We analyze things that we ought to simply appreciate for their beauty, and we miss the miracles going on all around us. We sometimes obsess over physical parameters in our lives—like our bank accounts, our weight, our cars, or our sports teams—instead of holding those things lightly. We would do well to notice and tap into the wealth of beauty, stillness and light instead.

From time to time, I am inspired with radical, new perspectives on life, and I started writing these ideas up as blog posts, short essays and other writings. Before long, I decided to gather them together into tiny books. Three tiny books became four as more ideas starting coming to me. The more I write, the more ideas flow.

This series of books explores the big concepts: Thought. Reality. Changing the world. God, All-That-is, Spirit or Source—all aliases for the same thing. Intelligence. Wellness. Communication. Relationships. I will build on simple ideas as I go, but don't feel like you must read the books in order.

Thanks for joining me on a profound journey of big ideas.

Watercolour Painting

I picked up a paintbrush, hesitating. I had not painted in a long time, since I was a child. I'd been hiding behind the screen of busyness, in a haze of adulthood. I decided to paint a scene, to make my life the way I wanted it to be.

My hand was unsteady and I couldn't seem to make the shapes and lines the way I wanted them to look. I kept touching them up, but each stroke interfered with the previous ones, layering over top, smudging in the places I wanted definition, and coming out blotchy instead of smooth.

I wondered what was wrong with me. Why couldn't I paint a masterpiece? Why was it so hard to paint a simple scene?

Then it occurred to me: what if it isn't my

technique that needs more work, but the very brush I am holding in my hand?

If I have a scruffy old brush, no matter how carefully I try to use it, I will not be able to make a smooth line. I can try to grab it harder, or try to control it better—to be master of my domain, to take control of my painting!—but that frayed brush will always create a scene that is scruffy looking. It will still be beautiful, but it will have rough, uneven edges.

If I have a smooth, high quality brush, I can create very clean lines and pure colour blocks. If I want to create detail, with some concentration and a steady hand, I will be able to place the tiniest line or spot of colour precisely where I want it. If I grip it tighter, it will not make me a better painter; I must keep my hand relaxed. I must take my time, allowing some colours to dry before working beside them; if I don't, the colours will run together. No matter what I do, my painting will be beautiful, just as the one made with the frayed brush is beautiful. However, if I clench the brush too tightly or try to rush things, it will not look quite like I wanted it to.

The brush is my attitude, and at any time I can choose a different one to make a new line or brush stroke to add to my life-painting. If my attitude is frayed, everything in my life will take on that tone, but I can choose a new brush—attitude—at any time, to make my life's painting look different.

How I see the world, how I interpret what happens to me, and how I interact with the people around me are *entirely dependent* on what paintbrush I am holding. Stephen Covey put it this way: "We see the world not as it is, but as we are."

If life is a painting, every brush stroke is permanent and the paper is infinitely large. I can paint whatever I want—there is no limit to the amount of paint I can use or the space I can take up. I must simply learn not to be afraid of the permanence of it—my actions cannot be undone. Since it is a mural of infinite size, no one stroke, however indelibly made on the Universe, is overly important. All the shapes and lines combine to create the image, and although I may feel that some things are mistakes, the image is truly beautiful. I could choose to moan about how these strokes cannot be undone or covered by new paint, or I can look for a way to incorporate those strokes I judge as mistakes into my painting anyway. Another option is to turn my attention to what I'm adding *now* to the impossibly big mural that is life.

~

Life is more art than science. What is strange to one is beautiful to another; no two people have the same eye for art. While some like bold colours, others appreciate a subtle palate, but it is all a matter of individual taste.

No colour is intrinsically bad; no tone is definitively awful. It is all a matter of opinion.

Much of what goes on in life between people is an exchange of opinions. You will find more peace when you realize that you alone can judge your own artwork, and others are merely expressing their opinions. If you judge your artwork to be ugly, messy or just plain awful, remember that all artists need practice before they become celebrated. Be easy on yourself. And if you practice and it's still a mess, remember Picasso! Art, and life, doesn't have to be "pretty" to have value.

Most importantly, know that no matter what your life looks like, it is a beautiful piece of artwork, always appreciated by Source. No painting detracts from the paper it is painted on. All life is an improvement on nothingness.

~

As **conscious creators**—manifesters of our

own reality!—we sometimes get overly concerned with tiny details, not realizing that it is our overall vibration that creates the circumstances of our lives. Details can be indicators, but when we become zoned in on them, we no longer see the incredible largeness of our existence—the infinite canvas.

Another side effect of becoming too detail-oriented is that we focus too much on the strokes we are making with our brush instead of remembering the larger picture. Many small brush strokes make up the picture, but no one stroke is so important that it deserves to be pondered, planned, or obsessed over more than all the others. Each one needs some care and attention but pondering too much can be paralyzing.

There is a dynamic balance between sweating the small stuff, planning the next move, and picking up the brush and getting on with the painting. I have found when I am too goal-oriented, I forget what brush I am picking up. I ignore what attitude I am doing things in, and that is the most important part.

There are many ways to do the same thing, and an infinite variety of attitudes to adopt, too. In this painting analogy, the good quality brush represents an attitude that you carefully select, after thinking about the results you want and the way you want your overall life to be. It is being thoughtful, kind, and intentional.

The scruffy brush represents an old attitude that you've had a long time. It is your default way of operating, based on long-held beliefs often so ingrained, you don't even realize what you're doing.

There is also a cheap, dollar store brush. Have you ever tried to paint with one of these blunt, plastic monstrosities? This type of brush represents attitudes popular in our culture: vaguely unhappy, dissatisfied, worried and opinionated (yet without many facts to back those opinions). You can use that brush if you wish, but your infinite canvas is for *you alone* to paint, so why not take the opportunity you've been given to create something intentionally?

Life is art. Every moment matters, yet there is a bigger picture to see. And it is always beautiful.

The Problem with Disney

It all started with cave paintings. The first time a hominid smudged some coloured mud on a wall, we started looking at things differently. Things that weren't alive. Things outside ourselves. Things that were static and long-lasting. Some of these paintings have lasted thousands of years, which makes them *very* long-lasting.

Zoom forward with me to the satellite TV era where we receive invisible signals from flotsam in space. Many of those moving pictures are of things that don't even exist, except in a computer hard drive somewhere—animation or CGI. That's the amazing world we live in!

Try to imagine a time before TV, one hundred or more years ago. With no screen time, people spent a lot more quality time together—in family groups, social groups and among neighbours. We got our morality and ideas about how the world works by following the social norms or reading the Bible. We used to watch those around us to learn how to be in relationships, but now we start out as young people pursuing a Disney romance, and as we get older, we switch to copying other couples we see on TV. It seems that in general, we get our guide for how the world works from Hollywood and Disney.

It all seems fairly harmless until we think about the deeper consequences. When I watch a lot of media, I forget that it's meant to be entertainment only. It is not a visual display of how the world really works. I wonder how many ideas I have adopted from entertainment that are colouring my views of reality.

Movies and TV can desensitize us to violence and trauma in the world; they can make us less empathetic. We may start to think about our lives as if they are media; we want to be entertained, informed, or get caught up in the drama. We want our personal lives to be full of romance, and we want our vacations to be glamourous. We don't like looking awkward in public, because someone might be watching us. We love hanging out with that funny friend of ours because he makes us laugh, but if he goes through a tragedy and isn't funny anymore, we don't know how to relate. Comparing our lives with movies, TV shows and commercials leads to chronic discontentment.

So perhaps we should all watch Disney/Pixar animated movies and nothing else. Surely they are pure and portray the world accurately! Unfortunately, they don't depict life correctly either. The usual plot involves the hero/heroine in some sort of trouble or on a journey with certain helpers and villains along the way. Perhaps there is a wrong that must be righted. Once it is, or the destination is reached, much celebrating, singing and dancing takes place. Isn't that exactly like life?

Of course it isn't. However, I think many of us have unwittingly made Disney stereotypes a part of our ideology. Men in moustaches are probably bad guys, for example. A friend who had worked at EPCOT Centre told me that Disney had a rule restricting male staff members from having any facial hair—they had to be clean cut in order for children to trust them. Disney openly acknowledged that they had created an attitude of mistrust of moustaches!

Disney movies teach us to keep our eyes on the destination. It doesn't matter how you get there, just take on each challenge as it comes and get to the party at the end. If you think about it, the best parts in life are always along the way! Have you noticed Disney movies never end with the hero/heroine's death at a ripe old age surrounded by children and grandchildren? The movie just covers a short time in his/her life. Real life is not just a series of episodes; we have to learn how to live in between the adventures or challenges. Disney doesn't teach that, so many of us kind of flounder on a daily basis, or seek/create drama.

Disney movies, like life, are full of challenges. We might be learning from Disney that we cannot rest until every hardship is conquered or overcome. Why not see them simply as experiences to have?

Every pretty girl is not a heroine, and every moustachioed man is not a villain. Every personal flaw is not something to be endured. Every time someone does you wrong, you do not have to seek revenge or compensation. The one you've labeled the villain does not need to be humiliated and their humanity stripped from them in order for the song and dance to begin. You could choose instead to ignore them and give them none of your energy. You could forgive them. You could accept your flaws! You could see each person as unique, valuable and interesting. You could *enjoy* the challenges.

> One problem with too much screen time is we miss opportunities to *experience life.* Many of us have lost the ability to just look at and appreciate a sunset, without wanting to take a photo and share it on social media—to tweet it to all our followers, post it on Friendbook, Insta-wham, and so on. Our desire to keep up with social media adds a lot of mental clutter, and we end up looking at a little screen instead of the whole, gorgeous sky! There is joy to be found simply being in the moment.

We are all absorbing ideas from the things we watch. If we're not careful, we can take the messages to heart and think that they describe the real world. Remember that you are watching someone else's view of things, from the outside, and few movies or TV shows are exceptions. Even news shows and documentaries which are not supposed to have a plot often have an agenda.

Looking at life from the outside changes everything. I believe magic is all around us, but it doesn't spring up out of nowhere in the form of a talking snowman. You must look for it and savour it, because although it is common, it is not to be taken for granted. Give up the screen. Look for the real magic.

Perfect Action

The paintbrush, or attitude, that we use when we approach life affects how we experience it. Over time, our attitudes can change, and this happens as a society, too. Before the 1970's, people viewed themselves as part of their neighbourhood and had a strong sense of community and duty. They had integrity and gained much of their identity from their cultural/family group. In the last few decades, there has been a movement towards individualism. For anyone in this generation, born after 1975 or so, self-esteem has been the main focus.

Young people today are at the peak of the change—the far end of the pendulum swing. They are more independent and entitled than any generation has ever been. They've been raised to believe that they are movers and shakers. In some households, everything revolves around what the kids want. A common message throughout society as a whole is that *you can do anything if you believe in yourself.*

As with anything taken to its extreme, this isn't exactly true. I have friends in this generation range that are finding they can't manifest all they desire, and they can't figure out why. It seems to me that putting your mind to it is not *quite* enough.

Make no mistake—the attitude you choose when you do something is crucial and your belief will shape the outcome. But you have to **do** something. Believing you can do it is not the only step.

There is power in the act of making a decision. That sets your course, and if you set an intention or imagine the outcome you desire at the same time, it will get you started in the direction you want to go. But you must still take action. There is more to it than imagining your success. You must go to your classes in university and listen to the professor, or take the course and do the practicum to learn a trade, or do the work to excel at your job. Take the next logical step towards your goal. Thinking you can do it is not enough; at the same time, acting without thinking is a sure way to tire yourself out. It tends to lead to frantic activity and a lot of unnecessary work. You must do both—believe in yourself and also learn how to be successful. Follow the advice of others and listen to your teachers. If you want to be an entrepreneur, then listen to what other entrepreneurs suggest.

You have to practice to get good at something—that's a universal truth. If you've been told you are amazing for your whole life, you may think you're a prodigy when you simply aren't. Practice will be required, and sometimes tenacity, problem solving and hard work. Growing up on the farm, I learned the Bible verse, "whatever your hand finds to do, do it with all your might" (Ecclesiastes 9:10) and made it into my mantra. This shaped me into a hard worker, but I wish I had also known the value of choosing my attitude. I got my self-esteem from a job well done, and to this day I have to remind myself that I have value even when I'm not productive.

~

Self-esteem is important, but it becomes a harmful attitude when taken to the extreme. Someone who *only* esteems him/herself would not have very good interactions with others. They would be disrespectful and cocky. They won't want to listen to anyone else's instruction or advice. They have fallen into the trap of self-esteem, and it will handicap their pursuit of success and happiness—and even relationships or friends.

Believe in yourself but keep some perspective. Remember that you are part of a larger community (more on this in Tiny Book #4 *Togetherness - Healthy Friendships, Relationships and Communities*). Visualization and action go hand in hand. Think things through, ask your intuition what seems best, and then take perfect action. This is how successful people do it!

Making Your Mark on the World

Have you ever heard of someone going to great lengths in order to leave his mark on the world? Some people have children as a way of leaving a legacy, and others want to build a giant sculpture or an enduring business empire. For many of us, leaving a mark is a deep, driving desire.

Our mark is like our fingerprint on the world. Sometimes we obsess about leaving our mark as if trying to squash our fingerprint into the medium of life—to leave a permanent mark so we can feel important, or so we won't be forgotten. We don't realize that our metaphorical finger has no ridges because nothing lasts forever. So, we strive to leave an imprint, to leave indentations in the clay, but the medium of life is more like a transparency.

Do you remember transparencies? They are clear pieces of plastic that teachers or professors write on and then project onto the wall behind them, so that everyone can see the concept they are trying to teach. They are thin, flexible and smooth.

What if our core identity is like a fingerprint, faintly showing on a transparency? When we want to leave our mark, we try to darken our fingerprint design. We trace over it with a marker, but as soon as it's dry, it starts to fade. So we trace it again. We obsessively try to make ourselves noticeable or unique. The mark fades immediately because it's impossible to be *more* unique.

At our core, in our true essence, our fingerprint—our personality, quirks, desires, dreams and everything that makes us who we are—is an oh-so-faint mark on a transparency that the light of Spirit shines right through. Our identity is a combination of our human uniqueness and Spirit or God shining through our humanness.

But surely we must be different than everyone else, right? We want to be special, with something special to show for it! Of course we do. However, there is no effort required, except to *be.* There is no work to do.

~

I think living up north changed me. I learned to be present by the mighty river and just watch it flow. I learned to get out of my head, and occupy the present moment with the Spirit of life pulsing through me. I learned to live without modern conveniences that add so much mind clutter. But it is very hard to un-learn a lifetime of working for self-esteem, thinking constantly and critiquing everything. Life is art, and it's also like going to the symphony—incredible music to hear, and musicians to watch and appreciate. It is feeling the sound of the tympani resonating in your chest. It is trying to figure out how the harpist does what she does. It is being in a field of possibility with everyone else in the concert hall, in awe and in love with the moment.

So, if I am an incredibly faint fingerprint on a transparency in an all-permeating field of Spirit, how can I live more fully? I simply need to be true to myself and remember that we are all learning to do the same. We are all impressions of Spirit. We are here to experience all aspects of life to the fullest—to allow Spirit to project its Light through our individuality.

As we near the end of our life, we get tired of obsessing and tracing that pattern on the transparency. We no longer want to darken it, so our body finally lets go—finally lets our spirit be light, be transparent, be the absolutely unique and utterly effortless expression of Spirit that we truly are.

~

If we are all transparencies in a pile, then we rub up against each other, don't we? Our family and best friends are closest to us, and our beautiful, intricate fingerprints line up, sometimes, and create patterns lovely and mind-blowing. They are like moiré patterns, like mosaics, or like the way a quilter stitches a pattern of leaves over top of a quilt that is already beautifully patterned and crafted.

Collectively, we are patterns on top of patterns—creativity on top of creativity. Rather than trying to leave a physical imprint with a stamp that has no indentations, we are happier when we allow our fingerprint, faint and lovely, to overlap with those around us to create patterns, harmonious and joyful, like beautiful art.

Here we are again, tempted to look at something as though we are not a part of it—like life is art behind glass, sealed in nitrogen and illuminated with carefully controlled light. We are *in* the painting, and it might be messy or wild, but it is beautiful.

I think we've all seen the carefully-crafted photographs of happy couples walking on the beach at sunset. Sometimes when we walk on the beach, we compare ourselves to that iconic couple, don't we? When we get caught up in thinking about whether we look like they do, we miss out on the whole ocean there, that we could be swimming in, splashing and playing in. We are immersed in ocean breezes, even if we are too out-of-the-moment to realize it. Whenever we are lost in our heads, Source is still there. We can never be outside of the air we are surrounded in; we can never be outside of Spirit.

You may argue this, saying that we humans have been outside the air we are surrounded in—we have a space station in orbit. We have flown the upper atmosphere. Perhaps my quaint analogies are out of date.

We live in modern times and we cannot deny that. No one really uses transparencies any more. So let's update this analogy. If your physical body is the vehicle for your consciousness, have you ever felt like you're in your little body of an airplane, flying in circles looking for the free Wi-Fi? Circling, checking for a signal, circling more... when instead, you could be using the fuel that is yours, for as long as you can make it go, to fly somewhere interesting and look around. Fly the Grand Canyon! Dip and arc, climb and bank that little aircraft, and look out the window the whole time. Wherever you go, *be fully there.* Occupy the whole space of your body, and claim it. Stretch its muscles and open its eyes. We are each given the airplane with a full tank of fuel; it's our decision how to use it. And every decision is the right one! Live fast and hard, if you feel like your plane is a fighter jet! That's your call, and it's absolutely one hundred percent awesome. Or fly your sleek little 2-seater, nimble and free. You can't do it wrong. There's no way you will crash, because you are never outside Spirit, any more than you could ever fly outside the Universe.

Release your need to leave your mark; allow Spirit to shine effortlessly through your unique humanness. Have experiences, don't just watch. Change the way you think about life, in particular, the future. There really is no future—there is only now.

Coloured Dots

Imagine a huge white wall, covered in coloured dots. For simplicity, imagine they are all perfect circles, and they appear in every colour of the rainbow; they are vibrating in every colour you can think of. They are interspersed randomly, with reds beside blues mixed in with shades of green and yellow. No colour is better than any other; they are just different.

Imagine that you are one of those coloured dots, and you are making your way from left to right through the field of dots. You can be whatever colour you want to be, but for today, let's say you are orange. As you go through life, you are sending out "orange" vibrations. You will pass by and between dots of all colours, and you won't interact with very many, but you will definitely bounce off or hang out with other orange dots. They are all tuned up to receive those vibrations, so you two will naturally hook up, whether it is in the form of a relationship, like a friendly checkout

An analogy for musicians: Imagine you are in a room full of tuning forks, all for different notes. They are standing upright, and if you wanted to, you could walk around the room and strike any one you like and hear its tone projected out. Instead, you stand in the middle of the room and sing a pure, clear note. The tuning fork that matches the note you sang begins to resonate. It begins to "sing" as well. That's how the universe works. What you focus on, you sing about. The notes you sing resonate in the universe—in particular, the way you sing them—and set up harmonics which bring experiences into your life.

lady at the grocery store, for example, or an amazing new job opportunity. It is the vibe of the thing/person/ experience that matches yours.

Suppose you decide that life is too hard and you're just going to stay in your rut and sit it out. You don't want to move through the field of dots. Well, no one is ever really standing still, and the other orange dots out there will still be attracted to you and find you. All those coloured dots we imagined at the beginning are moving, too. It's not a static field; everything is in motion, drifting one way or another. Think of it as a sort of nebula where each dot has its own trajectory/motion.

Although there are dots of every colour, you will only interact with the orange-ish ones. You may see some red ones, because orange includes the colour red, and you may have fun with some yellow ones, too. But as long as you are orange, you really won't see or feel the effects of the blue ones—you are blind to them. You will attract and be attracted to orange experiences. You will look at the world through an orange lens, be that optimistic, pessimistic, scientific or mystic.

So if we all attract similar colours, why don't all the orange dots clump together at one side, and all the blue dots in another area, and so on? The colours stay mixed because no one is orange or red or blue all the time. Not only are all the dots moving, but they are changing shades constantly. You know as well as I do that a day can start out mediocre and go either way—better or worse. We are constantly changing what we are thinking about and since our thoughts determine our vibe, our "colour" is constantly shifting as well. What we are attracting is shifting, as is what we are able to see/experience.

When you meditate, you "lighten" whatever colour you are vibrating in. You shift the shade. You connect with Source, so any darker emotions like jealousy or fear that you may have been feeling are eased.

Do we ever interact with a colour that just isn't us? Like an unexpected car accident, we may have an experience that we feel doesn't match our current vibe. We feel like we are orange, but in reality, we are often a muddy shade of brown, in transition from one colour to another, and we have many vibrations going on at once. In addition, if you went through many years of your life in a blue vibe, but you've set an intention to be more orange from now on, you may slip back into a blue vibe whenever you are not paying attention. You may have a blue vibe cloaked in orange now, so you think it's orange, and those around you see some hints of orange, but it's still blue.

For example, if I had been in a relationship where the two of us regularly judged each other harshly and played mind games, in a new one, it will be very hard not to slip back into that way of relating. With some time in between, single, and a change to a conscious way of living—always looking at myself when I feel an ugly emotion to see what the root of it is, and always stopping myself before acting on an unpleasant impulse—a new, healthy, beautiful relationship is possible. Without that time between relationships, to retune my vibe, I will still be giving off shades of disrespect and self-loathing, and the person I find will match, even if he/she seems very different from the last person.

Analogies built upon analogies, coated in examples! That's what it takes to understand how the universe works. After all, didn't Joseph Campbell say that God was a metaphor cloaked in a mystery?

When you have a car accident that you didn't see coming—literally or figuratively—the sooner you can accept what has happened the sooner you will be able to choose a new vibe. Some part of you was vibrating brown, so you attracted the crapola of a car accident (pardon the crude analogy). It is common sense, and even Hollywood depicts it right: you don't get in a car accident when you're cruising down the road with the top down, your best friend in the world beside you, the sun on your face and the breeze in your hair. You get into an accident when you are trying to finish your Christmas shopping on December 23rd, and you're rushing from one place to the next with a car full of crying kids! You might think your risk of an accident is the same any time you get behind the wheel, but if you are generally feeling good—feeling like the Universe is on your side and things are going your way—then things go smoothly. Bad drivers are not on your path, or they act unusually good when you're around. Sometimes, they'll pass you wildly (and without incident) and quickly move out of your experience.

We don't have a uniformly "good

experience" in life, in general, because we don't maintain a pure positive thought-vibe. Our colour is constantly shifting. We can have a more pleasant life experience, however, by becoming aware of our thoughts and choosing not to focus on the ones that make us feel cruddy—let those ones go with a minimum of energy. If we generally try to feel good, we can improve what happens in the overall trend of our life.

~

Becoming aware of our thought patterns, issues, and false beliefs is a good first step towards letting them go or transforming them.

Many of us have trust issues. We don't trust that God—Source, Spirit or the Universe, whatever we believe in—is on our side. Why would we? The image of God prevalent in our society is like a cosmic Santa Claus—he's watching us, taking a tally, and deciding who gets blessed with the gifts and who does not. Biblical views of God often depict him as a moody tyrant, blessing his chosen people and cursing others. Both views are so far from the truth! These paradigms reinforce a bipolar good/bad way of looking at the universe. The Universe is in fact made of every colour imaginable and it is all supposed to be there. God permeates it all, and it all belongs.

I know that idea is so counter-culture, I risk losing you to a swarm of distracting ideas. How can you say child abuse is supposed to happen? What about the holocaust? How can God LET those things happen? To this I say, how can WE let those things happen?! We are spiritual beings having a physical experience, here, now, and we have the ability to change the physical things in our world. We are in charge of this planet. To blame God as being absent, negligent or not caring is passing the buck, but I understand why people do it; it eases their own pain about why they, or others, weren't able to stop these bad things from happening.

I know I am asking you to take a very broad view of things, but it is the *Universe* we are talking about. I am asking you to question things you have been believing for a long time, to question things you heard on the news and morality you picked up from Disney movies. God is not like Santa Claus. God is in you; there is no separation. We are the hands and feet of God.

It all belongs. Brown is a colour, too, and life is supposed to have variety.

What about when a small infant or child goes through an illness, tragedy, or abuse? Did the child manifest these difficulties? I don't believe so. Small children "swim" in the vibe of their parents and their culture—even the vibe of the entire human race, to a degree. Their energy is deeply intertwined with their parents and closest caregivers; the adults in their lives do all the manifesting. Young children simply aren't responsible for the situations in their lives. When they get older—the exact age varies—they start to create their own life apart from their parents.

The Dark Side of the Law of Attraction

Before I knew about the Law of Attraction, I tried to do my best, but often felt tossed on the winds of fate—seeking God's blessings but not sure how to go about it. When I started really understanding that we each create our own reality, I realized that I was responsible for the state of my life.

When things are going well, we are happy to say we manifested it, aren't we? When we struggle with something, it's pretty hard to stay positive. We blame ourselves for not being able to make a better life. It should be as easy as thinking about what we want to attract.

The dark side—to borrow a term from

Star Wars—of the Law of Attraction is when we judge or blame ourselves or others for not being able to easily manifest what we want. We oversimplify it and use it as an excuse to be critical, rather than learning how to accept ourselves and our situation more lovingly.

~

Part of my problem is I tried to use the LoA the same way I was taught to pray. I asked for what I wanted. I pleaded. I asked in new and different ways, but generally with a sense of desperation. I focused on what was going wrong in my life and tried to change it. I did the same when I prayed for others. I felt bad about their situation and wished it to be better. The Law of Attraction is not activated by wishing, no matter how hard you do it. The vibe of "wishing" usually has too much strife in it. If there is a bad drought, wishing alone will not change it. Action is needed. The most impactful thing you can do is pray for rain, but you cannot do so with drought in the front of your mind; the Law of Attraction will bring more droughts. I have found it most effective to imagine the most glorious rain I have ever experienced—a slow, steady, soaking rain that goes on for days and days—and focus on that so clearly that I am reliving the event. I do this with the most abundant, appreciative, universe-trusting, happy and lighthearted feeling I can feel. This brings the rain!

It's not as simple as thinking about what you want. Our tendency is to think about what is currently going on—facts, statistics, and observations or news reports. If you lived in a drought-stricken area, you would have a hard time focusing on anything else, too. It is very counter-intuitive that the more you struggle against something, the more of that thing you will get. To use the Law of Attraction properly, you must think of what you want and somehow distract yourself from thinking about the existing conditions that you don't want. It often helps to accept what is and not fight against it. Then you can use your imagination to focus clearly on what you really want. As much as you can, conjure up the **feeling** that comes with the manifestation, and the highest vibration you can reach, such as appreciation and joy. In many cases, it is best to avoid getting overly specific—focus on the general feeling you are looking for. Sometimes, all you can do is distract yourself from the present conditions.

Accepting what-is allows us to relax about it, which automatically raises our vibration. Struggling against something keeps our attention on it—in a fight, you cannot turn your back on your opponent, right? You must stay focused on him/her. However, if you take a few steps back and walk away, the fight will very likely end (unlike fights you see in movies). At any moment in time, you have the option to choose to stop fighting something in your life—to believe that everything in your life belongs. You are exactly where you are supposed to be, based on what you have been thinking about, feeling, and expecting. It's not fate or predestined; you are where you put yourself, and it is not wrong or bad or terrible. It just is.

Believing that everything is as it is supposed to be does not preclude the possibility of growth or evolution. Anything can change in a moment. Change and growth are a part of life; they are in fact part of the **definition** of life. Anything that is alive grows. Anything alive changes.

Pendulums and Cycles

If life is all about change, let's look at some patterns in change. Some things in life change or move in a cyclical pattern and others are like a pendulum—they swing back and forth.

Things that are cyclical end up where they start; they repeat their path in a consecutive way. Their patterns are familiar, and they can be predicted; the seasons changing is a good example of this.

Things that are pendular back up on themselves; they end up at the far extreme from where they started, then vastly change directions, before returning to the previous place or state (although because life is always changing, they will never return to exactly the same place). In order to change directions, they must come to a stop. While they are in motion, change happens quickly. Examples are politics or the economy.

It seems that man-made things tend to be pendular and natural things are often cyclical. Energy vibrations such as those of the chakras are cyclical in nature, and in fact the word chakra means “spinning wheel” in Sanscrit. That makes sense, doesn’t it? I used to imagine pulsating orbs of different colours centered on the chakra locations, but in truth, there is rotation there. They have a cyclical nature.

If everything can be described as having cyclical motion or that of a pendulum, then what about things that seem to march forward? Could it be that things that seem to travel in straight lines are actually parts of very long cycles? Or cycles of another nature? Think of a river—it may appear to simply be a collection of water in a valley, running in one direction, but it is a crucial part of the water cycle. The water is not merely flowing toward a lake or ocean; it is also evaporating, forming clouds, and raining back down to earth. Any small portion of a circle viewed up close can look like a straight line. To see the curve or cycle, one has to back up, zoom out, and look for the bigger picture/perspective.

We nearly always think of our life's journey as a line that goes in one direction. We usually do not imagine it with any switchbacks, hairpin curves, or repeats to walk a section over. But if life is a cycle, from birth to death, then perhaps there can also be repeated sections or convoluted paths on this earthly journey, and it all belongs. Your growth is a cycle, and everything you experience is celebrated and savoured by the Source within.

There is also a lot of evidence for life cycles that repeat after death. In countries where a belief in reincarnation is common, there have been hundreds of documented cases of children remembering things from their previous lives—including details about events in the village—or being born with birthmarks related to their death in the previous life. There are too many occurrences of this to dismiss. It seems reincarnation is a cycle that we go through as well. We don't remember our previous life, generally, because it would be too much of a distraction for us on this one. There is enough going on here and now and our creative power—to decide the course of our life—is focused in this moment, not anywhere in the past.

The Power of a Word: Acceptance

The words we use when we talk to ourselves and others are very important, and it's the feeling the words create that we need to think about. The same word can create different feelings for different people. I mentioned acceptance in a previous chapter, so let's take a closer look at it.

Acceptance is often discussed in Zen Buddhism and some personal development circles, but it has a couple of different feelings behind it. For some, acceptance has the ring of resignation—it implies giving up on a struggle. Many people resist that concept, because ever since World War II our culture says to never give up—keep fighting no matter what.

However, without the correct use of imagination to picture or "pre-live" what we want to happen, what we fight grows. So, resigning or giving up the fight is the absolute **best** thing we can do, and that's why so many teachings focus on acceptance as a route to more contentment, happiness, prosperity and a thriving life.

If you want to tap into the power of the word acceptance, you have to come to peace with the word. You have to decide that your life is not a battleground, and that your purpose in life is not fighting against some theoretical "bad part" of yourself—an idea which is strong in our culture, too. We are expected to fight our "dark side," to never let it win, to conquer our shadow and so on. This way of thinking promotes a dualistic schism—that we are both good and bad, and have a devil on one shoulder and an angel on the other. This simply isn't true; remember the field of changing coloured dots? We are complex creatures, and we can pick up so many different ideas. It all belongs. All our thoughts belong. Some definitely should not be acted upon; they should just be allowed to exist for a brief moment in time and then be released. Some are better to just flow through or flow by us; we choose which ones to ultimately focus upon and make into our reality.

Reality is another word that many people misunderstand. Our society loves scientific thinking, so we tend to believe that reality is objective, can be measured absolutely and described accurately. But the describer—the person who is doing the observing—determines what is seen. There is no such thing as just one reality. It changes for each person and each moment. It's like we're all wearing rose-coloured glasses in one way or another—our attitude/vibe determines what we see and what we are blind to.

~

Let's look again at the word acceptance. For many, to accept a situation is to condone it, and when it comes to crime and injustice, the last thing we want to do is condone it. However, acceptance is not the same as condoning. Acceptance applies only to this exact moment. It means to see and know where you are, and what your internal state is. Acceptance might say, "yes, I am not in a very good place right now. I am hurt, and I am angry at the person who did this to me, the police who can't catch this bastard, and the world in general." Acceptance means that right now, you stop denying or fighting anything in yourself, your past, or your present. It does not have anything to do with condoning–judging what's right or wrong. Acceptance is simply recognizing where you are, and allowing yourself to feel whatever you are feeling.

Starting from a place of acceptance, you can choose the direction to go in. You can tell yourself, "I am mad about what happened. I am hurt. I don't want to be this way forever, but I'd like to be mad just a little longer." Then one day, you may realize you're not as mad, and mostly just hurt. Starting from a place of "yes, I'm in a bad place, and that's why I'm not happy," is better than not accepting where you are and mindlessly reacting to things around you, judging yourself harshly, and being angry about everything.

Perhaps the best way to think of acceptance is the opposite of denial. Denial is not a good long-term mode of operation; it is only necessary immediately after a trauma to give you time to process what happened. Try asking yourself, "what am I in denial about?" That's the thing you have the opportunity to accept.

Acceptance does not judge. It doesn't over-analyze. Acceptance has the feeling of being centered, like a dog sitting back on its haunches, calmly looking at its surroundings. The mantra "clarity, focus, ease, grace" (from Dr. Maria Nemeth's book *Mastering Life's Energies: Simple Steps to a Luminous Life at Work and Play*) has the feeling of being poised for growth, or movement, like a dog on all fours, deciding what direction to go next. All five words work together beautifully.

Acceptance. Clarity. Focus. Ease. Grace.

Perfect Place, Perfect Time

One August evening, I was in the right place at the right time to save a life. There was a tiny, young barn swallow caught in a piece of netting hanging from the eaves of the building where I worked. The netting had been installed to prevent the swallows from nesting there, but they had ignored it and built their nest on top of a security light nearby—it was the perfect nest platform. The young swallows had only been flying for a few days, and this little one had become tangled up in the net and couldn't get free.

One wing was up at an odd angle and I saw the swallow struggle sporadically, but it obviously couldn't free itself. I knew I needed to intervene, and although I was a little nervous, I was pretty sure I could help. I have handled birds before, like when I tried to save an evening grosbeak that had flown into my living room window, or when I was growing up on the farm. I often picked up fuzzy chicks, and although this little one had its flight feathers, it wasn't any larger than a chick.

I got my small-but-super-sharp scissors out of my knitting bag, just in case I needed to cut some of the strands of the net. One of the adult birds was sitting on a railing nearby, cheeping encouragingly to its young, so I steeled myself to be dive-bombed. The parents of this family had been very defensive, often dive-bombing me in a no-nonsense way. As I approached, the adult flew away and perched nearby. I prepared myself, calmed myself deeply, and walked up to the little bird.

It was too high. I had underestimated the height of the netting, so I hurried back inside to get a stool. Back at the little bird, calm again, I positioned the stool and stepped up.

That little fella was really tangled. I could

see part of the net wrapped around his left wing, which was why he was at such an odd angle. I reached up and started snipping at the net with my right hand. I realized I would have to cut him completely down to properly untangle him, so I started cupping the tiny bird with my left hand. There were threads wrapped around his body, tangled in his feet, and he couldn't move much at all. The chick was incredibly calm as I snipped away at the strands. He didn't flap or show any signs of distress, and the other members of his family were nowhere to be seen. I think they were all waiting and watching to see what would happen.

I kept snipping until I could lower the little bird to continue freeing him. I had to carefully cut and untangle the netting that was wrapped around and around his left wing. Finally, I had it all out. I lifted him up a little and we had a moment. He looked a little stunned, perhaps scared, but he wasn't panicky at all. Then I saw another piece of string coming out from under his other wing. I hadn't noticed it before because most of it was under his feathers, right against his skin. I pulled ever-so-gently on the end and untangled it—it was completely wrapped around his neck! He had been nearly suffocating while struggling in that net.

Now he was truly free. We had another moment. I looked into his little face as he looked at me. We made eye contact. He was so tiny! His body was much smaller than a ping pong ball. He was still completely relaxed and at ease. I smoothed out his feathers a little and gave him another look over, to be sure there were no other threads. He was good.

I gently set him down on the nearby railing. A breeze of wind caught him and he flew away, circled around and landed a little ways farther down the railing. Two chicks who had been silently waiting in the nest just above where I had been working started cheeping and took to wing. The adults joined in and the family of five rejoiced. I cut the rest of the net down so that entrapment would never happen again. As I walked back inside, they did a little air show of appreciation for me. Such joy!

I got to thinking after it was all over—what a good thing I was there when I was! I couldn't think of anyone else who works in that building more equipped than I was to rescue that little bird. I noticed at the perfect time that he needed my help, and the rescue went perfectly well. It was all so *perfect.*

Barn swallows have such a lovely spirit, and that tiny one was so grateful to be rescued. Those birds were my delight for the whole summer. I love how they dance in the sky, racing furiously around, testing the speed of sound, it seems. I watched them build their nests, with little balls of mud in their beaks, and saw the first fuzzy heads when the eggs hatched. I took photos of them huddled together on a rainy day, and earlier on the day of the rescue, I got a picture of three chicks perched on the edge of their nest, looking down at me a mere four feet away, very curious.

There are two barn swallow families, each with three chicks just learning to fly. They show such joy and gratitude at being alive, I don't think it's a coincidence that I was around to save one of them. Could it be that *they manifested me?* Their higher-than-high vibration manifested me being there at the perfect time with the perfect tool for the perfect rescue. And when it was over, we were all overjoyed!

It's an incredible experience to save a tiny life like that. I hope it wasn't a once-in-a-lifetime event; I would love to do that every day. I wonder if I could be at the perfect place/ time to help someone (or an animal) in the perfect way again. Because frankly, that was quite a rush. I feel like running away to join

Greenpeace to wash oil off pelicans!

So, maybe joining Greenpeace is not realistic. Where else could I be that perfect help? *Everywhere I go.* It has to be that way. *I am in the perfect place at the perfect time, to do the perfect thing, all the time.* Believing that changes *everything.*

~

I can no longer complain about anything. I can no longer grump about little things. It is easier to see the good in people around me. Every situation has a purpose; rather than bumbling along through life, I can now look around for how it can be perfect—how it *is* perfect. Where is my place in what is going on? Where is the vibrational resonance that made this moment happen? Is my place to raise the vibration a little to affect the outcome? Is my place to take a leadership role, and be the first to add perspective, forgive someone, or encourage someone? Is it time to simply exist and enjoy?

Believing that I am in the perfect place all the time means that I can't blame anyone or anything for an unwanted situation. If I knew it down to the depth of my being, I would not even be tempted to blame. I cannot indulge in even the slightest pity party for myself, or join someone in their self-pity. Believing in *the perfection of now* raises my vibration ever higher, without any effort. Judging a situation, blaming, or having pity only cloud my vibration, like a muddy stream flowing into a clear mountain river. Most of the water, my vibration, is clear, but sometimes, a little mud flows in.

Knowing that I am exactly where I should be really takes the pressure off. I no longer have to look for my purpose in life, or hope for that opportunity to make a difference in the world—it is everywhere I go. My purpose is to live each moment fully, as if it were perfect, and seize it as an opportunity to bring my unique, clear vibration to whatever is happening, wherever I am. It is simple; no career choice is wrong, no house less desirable, no friend less dear. Seeing the best in people comes naturally when you know that this moment is as perfect as it can be. It is the incredible culmination of exactly what I have been asking for—for many years, for my whole life.

A tiny, young barn swallow helped me see. Sure, I may have saved his life, but he gave me the realization that changed mine. As he did a flight-dance of joy for me, so I danced for him, and for myself. The next time I see him, we'll have another moment together, and it will be so sweet.

Dreams

I had the most amazing, vivid dream one night. I was a speaker at some sort of conference, and I thought I saw my dear friend Joyce standing at the back. Joyce is like a sister to me, and I had not seen her in a long time. It was such a nice surprise to see her there! A short time later in the dream, when I was done my presentation, a mutual friend brought her over to see me and we had an absolutely *real* hug. It was just the way she hugs, with arms wrapped all the way around and lots of squeezing. I could not believe it was not real! We laughed and cried while we hugged and I did not want to let her go—just the way a real reunion with Joyce would be. The whole dream was full colour, and she looked exactly like herself—nothing like those vague dreams I have where I'm not quite sure who I'm with.

No one knows what causes our dreams. If someone could create a pill that gives good dreams every night, they would be a millionaire. I wonder if my reunion-with-Joyce dream was caused by the rhodiola I started taking. It is a medicinal plant that's supposed to help with stress, anxiety, brain fog and physical and mental fatigue. It is also purported to help one have more vivid dreams and remember them. I didn't notice any difference that first night I took the rhodiola, but in the weeks that followed, I did notice that my dreams were more intense. I also wonder if my beautiful dream could have been caused by how lovely I was feeling before I fell asleep. I had snuggled with my husband for a bit and then rolled over and drifted off—happy after a great day at work and a fun evening of knitting. If I could prove that what I do in the hours before bed directly affects my dreams, I would be much more careful about what I do!

We all instinctively know about cause and effect. Like me wishing I could have good dreams all the time, we try to manipulate things in our lives by changing the causes. When I discovered the Law of Attraction, my eyes were opened to the fact that what I think about manifests in my life. So, I became a little paranoid about what I was thinking. Every time I had a negative fantasy—which I did plenty—as soon as I realized what I was doing, I would panic, thinking, "drat! I don't want that to happen! Quick, think about the opposite! Think about the opposite! Forget the other stuff." But it is so hard to forget about the other stuff. What I didn't know then is that my life is not simply the sum of my thoughts. We humans are complex, beautiful beings, a blend of our thoughts *and* feelings, and five seconds of negativity will not have any effect if my average way of relating to the world is positive. The problem was, after catching myself in the negative fantasy, that initial feeling of panic would linger. Even as I would try to turn it around, and long after I had moved on to a hundred other thought-topics, the panic was still there.

So many of us have this low-level anxiety because we have lost our sense of faith. I don't mean faith as it relates to religion. I mean that sense of faith that the Universe is not out to get us, that things will work out, and that there is love and beauty everywhere. We are so surrounded by bad news in the media, and we have become accustomed to thinking of God as "big, bad Santa." We seem to have personified the Law of Attraction and believe that it is out to get us too, and will bring every negative fantasy to life. It's very easy to become pessimistic and anxious living in this modern world.

I wonder if before we became so technological, when we as a society were closer to nature, we saw more balance. When a tree dies, there are always plenty of little ones to take its place. There are rainy days to balance out the sunny ones. There is wind to mix the air and snow to blanket the Earth against the bitter cold. I find that the more I am in nature, the more I feel assured and relaxed. I feel like Nature—Mother Earth, if you like—takes care of us. This planet is not just our home; it's our incubator, perfectly suited for us, for our growth and development.

Perhaps every aspect of our lives is part of that incubator. What if everything we are experiencing is carefully crafted to maximize our growth? What if everything is for our good, and we are perfectly outfitted to handle each challenge that comes along? What if everything we need to solve a puzzle or problem in our lives is already at our fingertips? What if every tool for the job is within perfect reach? What if the instruction manual is easy to follow and perfectly written for us to understand?

~

We can access this perfect instruction manual, or toolbox, in our intuition. In a quiet place, we can connect to a unique source of knowledge and tap into a deep well of wisdom. Wisdom is not just one-liners quoted by sages. Sometimes wisdom is a barrage of words, but often it is a quiet sense that cannot be put into words at all. Knowledge is not just facts; have you ever known something that, according to science, you should have no way of knowing? Have you ever done something without thinking, that you don't really know how to do?

There is absolutely no question in my mind that there is a deeper well we can tap into, easily, whenever we need or want to. We just need to remember that we aren't just brains on legs; our heart and our feelings matter too. When you are trying to use the Law of Attraction deliberately, focus less on the facts or the actual *having* of whatever you are trying to attract—less about the content or the plot of the fantasies you have—and more on the *feeling* of them. Focus on developing a **sense of faith in the universe,** that every tool is within reach, every problem easily solved. Life does not have to be hard. We make it harder by adding drama and agonizing over things we can't change. Yes, there will be things we can't change; the Law of Attraction does not prevent that. Some parameters are out of our influence, but we are always in command of how we respond to events in our lives.

Mankind will go on, doing his little things to manipulate the physical universe, while the *principles* of the Universe march on, never changing. Expansion. Growth. Newness. Beauty. Anything else is a blurry dream.

~

Dreams are one of those realms we can't even begin to explain scientifically. We barely understand why we sleep and we really don't understand what causes dreams.

The same is true for this dream called life. Although using the Law of Attraction seems simple enough, we may never figure out the details of it. How *exactly* can I replicate a positive experience I had? I can't. I am not the same person now. I'm a different colour. I'll never be in exactly the same place again. How can I replicate a positive experience *someone else* had? Impossible. I'm not them and the moment is gone. How can I prevent a bad dream from happening? There's no way to be 100% sure. Maintaining an overall sense of positivity, optimism, and cheerful anticipation of what life is sending my way gives me the best chance. Worrying about the bad dream and obsessing about it only brings down my quality of life.

Isn't it odd that we usually only consider quality of life for elderly people who are nearing death? How can we make their quality of life as good as possible for those final days? Why don't we ever think of our quality of life? We spend life-time as though we have so much to waste. It's okay if, for example, Monday to Friday we are miserable at work or spend hours stuck in commuter traffic. We never think of maximizing our quality of life for all seven days of the week. What if we looked at every decision through the "quality of life" lens? Will purchasing this new object improve my quality of life? Will this new activity improve my quality of life? I think it is an experiment worth trying—measuring everything based on the likelihood of it adding to our deep freedom and happiness.

Happiness and Expansion

Scientists pretty much agree that the universe is expanding. They have a way of analyzing the light spectra of distant stars and galaxies and it appears that nearly everything is moving away from us. Since it is unlikely that this is because of cosmic body odor, astronomers have concluded that the universe is expanding. Everything is getting farther away from everything else, not simply radiating outward from us or from some other central point. This is because the space between things is actually growing. Time marches forward and space marches forward, in a way. I don't want to lose you in the astronomical details, so let's simply say the universe is all about expansion.

So it occurred to me: what if we are all

about expansion, too? Our purpose is to grow, evolve and create things, and when we follow that path, we are in harmony with the universe we inhabit. Of course, life can still be cyclical within that expansion, with periods of joy and loss and everything in between, but overall, I think life is about expansion.

More evidence that this is a universal truth: we seem to be the most unhappy when we restrict ourselves, limit ourselves, or refuse to grow—in short, when we act against expansion. Wishing we could go back to the way things were in "the good old days" is a good example of acting against expansion. Of course it is tempting to wish for a simpler time and try to go back to it. We may also want to go back to old ideas, but it simply can't be done. We are all continually changing, and so is the world we live in. Trying to go back in time is acting against expansion and it breeds unhappiness.

Any sort of restriction interferes with our

happiness. When our budget is too tight or we feel like someone is controlling our time (like our boss), we feel frustrated. It doesn't matter if the restriction or limitation is self-imposed or from outside ourselves—or if it is real or imagined. The result is the same.

The universe is expansion, growth, newness and beauty. Doesn't that explain babies?! They are all those things. It explains why there are so many souls wanting to become human that they can't wait to incarnate into a tiny, crying baby. It is the most delicious experience—even the crying part—because it is an experience of expansion, growth, newness and beauty in a physical existence.

~

Think about what each of those words means to you: expansion, growth, newness and beauty. To me, expansion is similar to evolution, personal growth, and even reminds me of ways that technology is making our world more efficient. Expansion is being open to opportunities and new experiences. Growth makes me think of gardening, which also brings beauty into the world—and sometimes vegetables. I've heard that gardening is an excellent way to counteract stress and connect to nature. Creating something beautiful with your hands is fulfilling because it is tapping into newness and beauty. Whether it is knitting, crocheting, sewing, sculpting, painting, writing, playing music, writing a computer program, woodworking or restoring a classic car, all these activities are sources of newness. There is even newness in a room that's been tidied up or organized. Beauty is different for everyone, of course; to me, it is the interplay of colours in a sunrise or sunset, wild roses, or autumn in the forest. But it's also someone wearing no makeup at all, being themselves; it's almost anything homemade, whatever the skill level. These are just a few of my ideas; I'm sure you have your own. Really focus on those principles and how you could emphasize them in your life.

Go forward with expansion, growth, newness and beauty on your mind and you will see how easy it is to live in harmony with the universe.

Contradictions and Sleep

This world is full of contradictions. We grow grass, which creates oxygen and is good for our air quality, and then mow it with gas-powered mowers, which does the opposite. We need tourists for our economy, but we bad-mouth them. We know we ought to listen to our hearts, but we never do. Our hearts say to be compassionate towards others, but our heads want to analyze them. We get tired in the evening and need to go to bed, but we stay up doing some unfulfilling activity like watching TV or surfing the web.

Why do we do this to ourselves? Why do we do things we know will make us feel bad? We feel exhausted the next day and we feel bad emotionally because we know we are mistreating ourselves. I think we play this stay-up-late game because we are punishing ourselves. What for? It would be so easy to do the right thing and give ourselves the rest we need—so why don't we do it?

Sleep is such an odd thing. It's like who-we-really-are leaves our shell of a body for a while and goes... where? Why? It's not hard to figure out that we need physical rest to recuperate, heal wounds, and even for our bones to grow (in children and teenagers). Scientists recently discovered that our brains produce waste products when we're awake, and when we sleep, our brains contract slightly in size which allows fluids to wash it—to flush those wastes out. We can't stay conscious while this happens. But why do we need to sleep on a metaphysical level?

We are more than our thoughts, and our consciousness resides in more than just our brains. We get hunches, gut feelings, and other odd sensations that make me think that our consciousness is throughout our bodies.

Every cell has its own intelligence. Consciousness is much more than thinking. It is having an awareness of what-is, yet it is more than just being awake and receiving sensory input. It's that sense of awe we all get when we see majestic mountains. It is the feeling that something greater is present when I appreciate a beautiful tree. It is knowing that I am not the same as I was and that I can choose who I want to be.

Could it be that our consciousness needs time to rest too? It seems odd, but we might need a break from this human experience at times. We might need a chance to remember our godliness, to forget this temporary shell we put on and remember the Infinite.

How much time do we need? How does time even relate to this? Time is a dimension that applies to the temporary shell, not the infinite. We only need an instant to remember our godliness, and we can learn to do this in our waking hours. It turns out that feeling tired has far less to do with how much sleep I've had or how much physical activity I've done. I feel better when I relax and let go of the resistance I have been carrying around—this is the visualization that works for me. Have you experienced being exhausted at work only to get a new burst of energy when you get home and start doing something you enjoy?

We definitely do need sleep for physical reasons, but we also need it for spiritual ones. Our consciousness, or spirit, needs to reconnect to capital-C Consciousness, to Source. For most of us, living in the illusions and contradictions created by modern society creates pervasive resistance to the good that wants to fill our lives. We need to take a break from the negative thoughts we think—in particular, feelings of lack, inadequacy and shame that we get from functioning in society and from the hurts in our lives.

We are such a profound blend of spirit,

chemistry, and activity. There are environmental factors that make it easier to be more conscious and live in the moment more. There are chemical factors—what we eat being a big one—that make it easier to connect to Source and feel more at-ease. There are activities that send signals out loud-and-clear to the Universe that you want to connect to something higher, to know your infinite nature. There is a time for action and a time for non-action. Sit down somewhere quietly, every day for a month, and ask yourself what that is—what all those factors are. Ask what would maximize your quality of life right now. Ask how you can stop punishing yourself.

When we sit quietly, we get answers. I have found the best answers come when I first wake up. It is like Source is able to speak to me more clearly when I am barely awake, because my consciousness is not embedded in my physical shell so deeply.

Be prepared for interesting, profound and sometimes surprising messages, and whatever they are, listen to and act on them to the best of your ability. Use them to accept yourself more. Put a pen and paper at your bedside so you are ready to write them down exactly as they pop into your head.

> Do not get too concerned with trying to understand why you do things. Those answers are complex, and they will come through in small pieces. When we ask *how* we can make a change in our lives, we start to get new ideas. Spend time thinking about what kind of life you want to live. When you express a desire to live more consciously, more lightheartedly, more freely and more fully, the ideas that come are beautiful and lovely. It is difficult to describe! The more you act on the inspiration that you receive, the more will flow to and through you.

Be open to new ideas from Spirit. Above all, accept yourself.

Fear and Freedom

When something bad happens, we want to know why. We look for a big stick to hit someone (or ourselves) with. We can be tempted to blame ourselves for misusing the Law of Attraction to make this bad thing happen.

Here's a different approach, and it's the best way I know to tackle the question of why. Imagine you have a little-kid scientist inside you, who is happy and curious about the world and why things happen. Let him/her ask "why could this be happening?" with pure curiosity rather than dropping into a depressed adult response or descending into fear.

If you took a pigeon, those lovely, pleasant birds we see around us, and tied one to your finger, it would be terrified. Why?

Because you took its freedom away. If you instead befriended a pigeon and it came to rest on your finger, it would not be afraid because it knows it still has its freedom.

We are the same. We become afraid when we think that someone or something has taken our freedom away. It scares us. We want our freedom all the time; that's why we have police, laws, courts, and jails that *take* freedom. The fear of losing our freedom is supposed to keep us from breaking laws and interfering with each other's freedom.

We want freedom at all costs; that's why we'll bust our buns working for years and years, taking overtime shifts or switching jobs for higher pay, so that we can have more freedom when we retire. It's the promise of future freedom that keeps us going.

We want freedom above all else, and when we think our heroic efforts are going to fail, we become depressed and rebellious. Why can others have it but not me?

The idea that we don't have freedom—or can't have it, or that someone or something can take it—is an illusion. *Freedom is absolutely inherent to our being.* Life on this planet simply *is* free. That's why life is so interesting!

> Do not let jadedness about one thing take over your life. Do not let a breach in trust in one area of your life bleed into all areas. Learn to trust the Universe, Source, physics, Mother Nature, or some other higher power that makes sense to you. Any of these things will not let you down.

When you feel afraid, ask yourself if the fear is about freedom. Then remind yourself that *you are already free.* You are absolutely free to choose how to live. You are absolutely free to choose what thoughts to focus upon. In every moment.

Thoughts are floating around, like a cosmic buffet. You choose which ones to heap onto your plate, to devour or savour. Think of your brain as an antenna that receives impressions or thoughts, and you control the tuner for the antenna. When some new event happens in your life, you decide which thoughts to have about it, and you can choose a radical thought if you want to.

As we grow up in society, we are sort of programmed for the usual responses, like a laugh-track in a sitcom. We laugh at the jokes or situations that are supposed to be funny. When we are immersed in modern media, we may also be programmed to respond in anger, indignation or despair based on events that happen. Step outside the normal programming and start creating a vibrant, peaceful world by choosing your thoughts and actions more consciously.

~

One unexpected negative side effect of

the scientific revolution—the way that science has crept into every part of society—is that we have become quite analytical about **reality.** We want to measure things, inspect or observe things, quantify and describe things, and generally try to get a good handle on the objective reality of the world around us.

The problem is, we get so caught up in examining **what we see** we forget that we have the power to imagine what we want and **change our reality.** We tend to take our analysis down a pessimistic road; this makes us more likely to get into a downward spiral. We also forget that as the observers, we change reality just by looking at it.

For a while, I've had the feeling that as soon as I look at my dog or my Dad's horse, they know it. They can sense they are being watched, and they change how they behave. We are the same, are we not? We know when someone is watching. But why would a horse change what she's doing as soon as I look at her?

Does she do this because humans are so special? Is my attention all that amazing? It turns out, I think it is, but not in an egotistical way. I just think that we humans have a way of focusing intently on something and therefore changing it, just by our observation. Animals are not the same; they do not have the power of attention we have. I don't believe they have our power of *intention* either. When we add an intention to our attention, we can really affect the world around us. The limits are simply in learning to focus and to set clear intentions.

Reality Bubbles

Manifesting things is like shifting my position in the universe. My reality is a single bubble in a giant bathtub full of bubbles, yet to me it's the only bubble. I can't see outside it. However, it is touching many other realities on all sides, and I can jump to a new one by changing what I am thinking about and how I am feeling. I can align with any point where my bubble touches the next—which is infinitely everywhere and yet a discrete set of conditions—and move into that new reality.

If I want more peace and less stress, I can move into an adjacent bubble where my reality has those things. I would love to live in a world where people are compassionate and helpful, so I often think about moving into that reality bubble where others of a similar mindset live.

Far away from my bubble, there are realities that are very different from mine. There are an infinite number of bubbles between my current reality and those far away, but one tiny step at a time, I can move towards or away from them. If I consistently think about one I do not want to live in—where people are cruel, for example—I will jump from bubble to bubble until I end up there. The Law of Attraction says I cannot move **away** from anything, because I always move towards whatever I focus on. That is why watching the news is dangerous; we can inadvertently end up in a world with more crime or violence because we've moved into that bubble.

So, if I don't want to live in a cruel world, I can focus on being loving, forgiving, kind and gentle, and that will be my reality. Using a set of Virtues reflection cards or taking a Virtues course can be helpful for learning to focus on positive aspects you want to enhance. (For more information on The Virtues Project, see thevirtuesproject.org.)

The key is to choose with intention what direction to go in, rather than letting events in your life take you somewhere like a piece of driftwood tossed on the waves in the ocean.

Consciousness and Death

I've been thinking lately that movies often seem to have hidden meanings—a deeper message hidden within. In many Star Trek movies, there is a message about the profound friendship between people who seem to be very different—Kirk and Spock. In the classic Star Wars, epic battles between good and evil take place, based on two aspects of "the Force."

In quite a blinding flash of insight, I realized something profound about the nature of consciousness, and there's an excellent analogy from the movie Avatar.

In James Cameron's vision of the future, man has invented technology that allows him to psychically enter an avatar and live life through it. Humans, like the hero Jake Sully, connect to an avatar through a neural interface that allows them to receive sensory input from and control the Na'vi body, experiencing everything it feels.

Life on Earth is very similar.

There is a spark of life within each and every one of us that makes us *alive.* This essence of life, which we may call the *soul, spirit* or *life force* is Source or God living through us, animating us. Like humans using Na'vi avatars, Source comes into a human body to live life fully and experience everything it means to be human—joy, tears, happiness, pain, love. Source feels everything because it has the perfect "neural interface." When we lose consciousness—are asleep or meditating deeply—we partially return to the realm of Source. When someone dies, the spark leaves the body completely and goes back to the realm it came from. In *Avatar,* when a person such as Jake disconnects from the system, the avatar body goes limp, but the spirit that occupied it is not gone, it's just not animating the body at that time. Jake is still alive; he is back in his original state of being human.

When our body dies, the essence of who we are does not die. Our consciousness is an extension of Source. We are tendrils of Spirit, extended into a physical body for a time to experience love, create things, and grow through all our life experiences. These bodies were not meant to last forever; they are temporary homes for an eternal Essence. When our body dies, our Spirit instantly goes back to the higher plane from which we came. Our spirit harmoniously rejoins others like it, but can still see what is going on in the physical world and interact with it if we choose to.

This physical life is so intense, we don't usually remember the spirit realm we came from, but make no mistake—it is real. And it is full of love and joy and appreciation! Death is nothing to be afraid of. Fear of death consumes so many people, but death is just like falling asleep and waking up in another place—a familiar, peaceful place... like home. It is just like Jake disconnecting from his avatar (except without waking up in a strange pod). I also wonder if the fear of death is related to a fear of **life**—don't be afraid to live fully and let others do the same.

Notice that I didn't say "if you believe in Jesus, if you're born again, or if you do A, B, C and D," or any other conditions. That's because I don't believe there are any conditions—this is simply the way the world works. It's true for everyone, like physics. I believe peace and love are at the end, for all, no matter what. I've believed this for a long time, but I realize that it isn't this way for everyone. I think the Catholic church invented purgatory and hell and the fear of it (and by association, death) as a way to control the people. Well, the gig is up, and it is time to leave these old, false ideas behind.

Death is Nothing to Fear, Mostly

It is easy to say death is nothing to fear, until you face it up close. There is a very intense physical response when you actually think you are dying that is overwhelming to even the most enlightened among us. At the end of a particularly suspenseful movie, in which all my emotions were engaged, I had a sensation that made me think I was dying. I felt a pulsation in my abdomen—a thoroughly strange and alien sensation—and my advanced first aid training told me that it was an abdominal aneurysm. I've been trained that if you see a pulsating mass in someone's abdomen very carefully and quickly get them to hospital because if the bulging artery bursts, they will die within minutes. Patients who have had an abdominal aneurysm rupture while on a hospital operating table have still died because the bleeding was so severe. There is nothing anyone can do to help, but as a medic, it is still best to get the person to a hospital.

This pulsing is what I felt, very distinctly, in my abdomen. I knew what it was and knew the end was near. For several minutes while the movie credits rolled, I closed my eyes and felt a profound sense of peace and contentment; I really have lived the life I wanted to live and have no regrets or unsaid words. However, as the minutes ticked by and I did not die, I started to worry.

When would it happen? I was a little hungry; should I eat something or not? What would happen if I collapsed right there in front of my husband? How would he cope? He would probably panic and freak out. There was definitely no way to get me to a hospital quickly enough if that artery ruptured—I would bleed to death internally.

We went out for a bite to eat and I felt ill. It could happen any time! When would it be?

It was still pulsating frequently and I knew it was unstoppable. Death was truly inevitable and close at hand.

I didn't know what to do. Should I tell Darren? He might insist on taking me to the emergency ward, which was the last place I wanted to be on a Friday night, let alone my *last* night. No, I did not want to go to the hospital. There was nothing they could do anyway, except take pictures of it, and that was risky, too. It was a ticking time bomb in my gut, and I could feel every tick. The agony of not knowing what to do was far worse than the symptoms.

I finally decided not to tell Darren. I was freaking out most of the way home, and once in bed, I seriously wondered if I would wake up the next morning. Dying in my sleep would be okay, but was I *really* ready? Darren could tell something was up—I was ashen and tense. I struggled to maintain some sense of calm, against a backdrop of rising panic.

I told my honey how much I loved him. I thanked him for everything. And before very long, I fell asleep.

I was pleasantly surprised when I woke up the next morning. I was given another day. Before noon, I told Darren what was up and we agreed not to involve any doctors. The first few times I sneezed or bent over to tie my shoes, I held my breath to see what would happen. To this day, I feel the pulsing occasionally. It is more noticeable when I am hungry, but if I pay attention to my gut, I can feel it often.

So, I lived for over a year with a live gut-grenade,* waiting for it to go off. It made me a little more philosophical, frankly, and perhaps a little more qualified to speak of death and the preciousness of life. I am more aware of the universal truth that we can die at any time. I am more careful about how I spend my time. I pet my kitties, do far less email, and spend a lot of time outside. I know that the

Intelligence that makes me conscious, lives in me and loves every moment, even the stressful, agonizing ones. Being in a physical form is glorious, and being in one that has the ability to focus and give attention to things, even more so. From that eternal perspective, nothing can go wrong. Each moment is precious, delicious, and contributes to the expansion of the cosmic consciousness.

There is nowhere else I'd rather be, and I hope you feel the same.

*I did eventually go to my doctor and he ordered an ultrasound. Apparently, there was nothing unusual there. Another mystery!

About the Author

Teresa Griffith draws inspiration from nature and shares stories from her life on a small farm in Canada. She has also written *Love Your Skeletons,* a guide to overcoming painful or embarrassing skeletons in your closet, and *York Boat Captain -- 18 Life-Changing Days on the Peace River.*

In her series of Tiny Books on Big Ideas, she shares revolutionary principles and observations of how the universe works, the roots of happiness, connecting with profound intelligence, and deep, inspired wisdom on relationships with others and ourselves.

For more information or to contact Teresa, visit teresagriffith.ca.

www.ingramcontent.com/pod-product-compliance
Lightning Source LLC
La Vergne TN
LVHW010933110826
845149LV00013B/2583

* 9 7 8 0 9 9 2 1 2 0 4 1 2 *